T0125497

TO LOVE THE COMING END

Leanne Dunic

Chin Music Press
Seattle, Washington
Spring 2017

Published by:
Chin Music Press Inc.
1501 Pike Place #329
Seattle, WA 98101
www.chinmusicpress.com

First (1) edition

Cover design by Mallory Jennings
Interior design by Carla Girard

Printed in the USA

Library of Congress Cataloging-in-Publication Data:
Name: Dunic, Leanne, 1982- author.
Title: To love the coming end / by Leanne Dunic.
Description: First edition. | Seattle, Washington : Chin Music Press, 2017.
Identifiers: LCCN 2016056578 | ISBN 9781634059657 (paperback)Subjects: | BISAC:
LITERARY COLLECTIONS / Canadian. | LITERARY COLLECTIONS / Asian.
Classification: LCC PR9199.4.D864 A6 2017 | DDC 811/.6--dc23LC record available at
https://lccn.loc.gov/2016056578

ISBN: 978-1-63405-965-7

for r.

SIN. After worrying that a stranger has planted drugs on you, that you will be found out and sentenced with the death penalty, after, the next thing a visitor notices upon arrival is the fastidiously clean airport. Inhale. A verdant flora wall towers over the customs gates, absorbing carbon dioxide, releasing oxygen. Exhale. A full day of travel has come to an end. A sterile taste settles in the mouth, a hint of humidity on the arm.

This November features a series of elevens: 11-11-2011. Slender ones paired with their likeness. Posed together and apart, forever parallel. Is one still the loneliest number, or is it eleven? Only you and I can see this significance, the curse of 11.

When you and I were born on the 29th, which one of us said *jinx?*
$2 + 9 = 11$. We can't escape.

November: our birth month. Late autumn, we are. When dark comes early.

In Singapore, there is no need to hoard daylight. Year round, the sun rises and sets at nearly the same time every day. The seasons are unchanging—maybe a degree or two cooler or warmer, maybe more or less rain. I'm here for two weeks, promoting my book *Performing Asian* at the Literary Festival. I haven't practiced my presentation aloud. Who needs to prepare? I talk about this shit daily.

I listen to the radio to immerse myself in Singaporean music. Every station plays the same song by Rihanna. My fingers hurt from opening too many beers. No matter how many I drink I am not cooled in this heat. I've become a distended porpoise.

Respiration is forgetful.
Circulation refuses my hands.
Pain in my skull is equatorial.
Wake with vessels broken in my ear.
No cocaine, but heart palpitations.
Jaw is fixed.
Walk, toes curled.
Denude cells like a mountainside.
Skin births freckles worth watching.
Strands of bitter brown turn to bone filaments.
The cinch of a muscle bends me in half.
Shoulder is electric.
Eardrums resound frequencies.
Eyes closed, I see music in black and white when
we all know there is no such thing.
Ribs restrict the ability to sing.
Memories become dreams, and dreams are
where I peel dry sections of lip.
Sleep leaves imprints of fingers round my neck.
Looking behind is a physical impossibility.
Why my tail still twitches in your hand.

Dentist: *Do you wear your mouth guard every night?*
Doctor: *These ailments—stress.* Chiropractor:
Torsion. Tension. Relax. Massage Therapist: *You
need a counselor, not an RMT.* Counselor: *Not
stressed, sad.* Heart: *The work is too much.*

I hate November. Especially in Singapore. I've given up on aging, on anniversaries. I've given up on freshness. Showers are pointless when you step out of the bathroom and into fortified humidity. Despite the heat, I leave the flat to gorge on noodles oiled with meat fat and yeasty goods from BreadTalk. I'm readying for tropical hibernation.

I try to count the russet-colored panels on the fan pinwheeling above me. I'm unable to anchor the fan's moving parts to tally them. My body is still—at least, I think it is. Who can be sure of anything? A chrysanthemum shadow plays behind the fan, while two bobbled chains sway below the lights. The fan spins silent. I question its stability.

Beside me are the pills I never took. You gave them to me, promised me they would take me places. Now, the pills are all that's left, and they expired two months ago. This humidity hasn't helped their longevity. I wonder about their potency.

If I were to ever make a film, it would be set in Japan:

Nauseating speed of the Shinkansen. Inside train, camera turns to eyes that dart side to side, trying to compute rice field streaks, rivers, and peaks—the world passing at incomprehensible speed.

Even while in Japan, my missing doesn't thin.
Maples and pines root my muscle, call me back
to land.

It was there that you and I collided, and, of course, it was November. November 11th to be exact. Remembrance Day. I was researching the WWII Banzai Kamikaze attacks (note: 'two' marked with Roman numerals, resembling eleven). You were filming that music video with the murder-suicide ending.

World War II, Japanese temple bells were repurposed into weapons.

There was that saying I came across about the gyokusai. *A great man should die as a shattered gem rather than live as an intact tile.* An idiom that traces to the days of samurai, and further back to the Ming Dynasty. A strong sentiment among the youth of the Red Army.

In an interview, Yukio Mishima offered the opinion that Japan had two contradicting characteristics: elegance and brutality.

Carnelian and rust-colored maples frame a restive
volcano, exceptionally symmetrical. Highest crest,
branches bare, clouds. Snow-capped, flanked by
cherry blossoms. A melted tip veined with white.
They say Fujisan is ready to blow.

Former fears: a catastrophic earthquake, and for us to be apart.

MRT to the last stop, switch to the monorail to Sentosa Island. Ride alone past the thirty-seven-meter-tall Merlion, Singapore's myth and symbol. Unable to see its ichthyic tail from above, only its enormous maned head. It's too early to be here, but I want to evade people, heat. The maintenance crew collects fallen fronds, an excavator perfects the manmade shore. Stroll past the stretch of deserted beach bars, take off flip-flops, wade into the Singapore Strait. Sea organisms prick my calves like needles.

Seah Im Food Centre before the lunch rush. Order lime juice and roast duck rice. Auntie approaches my table offering tissues for sale. I gulp my drink. She holds three packets together, *one dollar.* I try my best Mandarin: *Bu yao.* She holds the tissues closer to my face. A Malay man at the table next to me: *Not aggressive enough. Bu yao! Not buuu yaooo.* I nod, try again. Short tones. She walks away. A rat scuttles under tables. Here, filth finds a place to rest, if only for a moment. My duck grease arrives. Spoon rice, meat, chili. Lift shirt to nose. It's too early to smell like fried cockles. At the fruit stall, rambutans, papayas, and mangoes ripen to rot, their flesh liquefying to sugary slush. Flies consider their options. I consider ice chendol. My lips are oily from lunch but the auntie is no longer here.

Scene at graveyard. Shot implies the possibility of
death, the chance of supernatural to come.

Remember eating lunch at that cemetery in Tokyo because there were no parks nearby and we had our FamilyMart sushi in hand? After, we harmonized that scene from *This Is Spinal Tap* like we weren't scared.

Gladwell says babies born at the end of the year are disadvantaged, that they are physically weaker compared to the babies born in the first half. According to the studies, growing up, you and I had to try harder to catch up to the successful Januaries and Februaries. I don't think we ever did.

To kill birds with stones. I must present at the Literary Festival, and, establish my next project. My Singaporean publisher wants the new book to be *sexy*, not like my previous work on the thriving wildlife in Korea's DMZ. Something akin to my exposure of the wondrousness and illegalities of Kowloon's Chungking Mansions.

Electric fans. Ceiling fans. An open window in the morning. I despise the pseudo-cool of AC. I step outside to test if the air is better. There is a pool in the courtyard, the surface blinding. Frangipani-perfumed air, sun-singed arms. Beyond the entrance I tread onto a tacky pink gob. Stuck to my sole. Illegal to sell but not to chew. I drag my sandal along the concrete. Cats pile in the shade next to me. They squint. It's cooler in the ditch.

Within me, a gaping crevice. The more I change my environment the more I lose track of myself, yet I traverse. Maybe that's the point. Nothing is anchored. Today is unstable, easy for people and land to split. Minerals grind a geological dance, the balance of the earth's axis shifts. Chile, Indonesia, New Zealand, Haiti, Japan. Where next? The unsure crust hectors the Pacific Northwest, evidence of instability buried under substrate. A story, mounds.

Volcanoes circle the Pacific. Enamored with its terrestrial beauty and sea, British Columbia forgets it lies on a restless coast scattered with summits of hardened lava, pumice, volcanic ash. Imagine, a seismic rip. Plates warp, lock, pull. Instant fractures. After, shocks. In the horizon, a wave emerges. A white line becomes a mountain. Surge and retreat. Thunder and silence. Sirens. Rush of the wave's return. Grab, toss, suck, slam, sweep. Ghosts swarm, a floating world.

Remember the days when I became a rhizome, a thing under your surveillance, something to cultivate? I was obsessed with being able to grow, to create an ideal environment for you and I. I tried to give you attention without possession. I felt the lust of science and soon, you became the subject. I studied you, no longer the root. I gave you soil. You said the conditions weren't right. *That's reality*, you said. Reality was a synonym for misfortune. I should have started the pills then.

There are many types of flora in Singapore. Parakeet flowers, orchids, bright flashes of red and hot-yellow. Sculptural foliage, umbrella palms, and frangipanis. Different climate, different kinds of life. I haven't gone to Jurong or to any of the reservoirs to explore nature. I don't know how to care for plants. How to care for living things.

Moist mountainsides, lush terrains for new shoots.
Bamboo forests, a landscape of jade green and
celadon. Variegated leaves rustle a game of telephone.

Singapore grows, a city of glass, as if there is no threat of plates and quakes.

On top of sweaty sheets, I exist without basic order. Order of eating. Of hydration. Of relieving myself of concentrated urine. Buddha says: *Existence is suffering. Desire is suffering.* To be awake with one's anxieties is suffering. If I can sleep, then I can survive, but there's something I desire, something that, in my rest-deprived state, seems attainable. Reunion. Perhaps through dreams? But then there would have to be sleep. Without worry, without unnamed guilt.

Reality is unreality. I have no references to validate my existence. Mornings and nights I pray to other gods, talk to you, think of new superstitions.

5 a m, I wake. *Hello?*

I haven't seen any mosquitoes, nor have I been bitten, yet throughout the city there are ads warning of dengue fever. *Do The Mozzie Wipeout. Our Lives. Our Fight.*

In my dream you declare, *I'll always know where to find you.*

Fault, when masses of rock have moved past one another.

If I gave this man my spine he'd grunt while forcing shoulders back. Mumble that I sit too much, unaware of where I've been, where I'm trying to go. Instead, he knuckles tendons, tender arches. Sole maps disclose memories, habits, nerves distended from fissures within. Stimulate crystal pointed organs, glands. A vast unnerving. Reflex, I contain. Yes, I'm deceptive—in voluntary restraint. Hand shields eyes as if it could quell throbs. Air-conditioned chills. Heat swells, cold brittles. *Good Morning* towel spread, I cross arms (such positioning why I sleep with fists). Mah-jongg tiles click from the room beside. Whine of ache drowns the chirp of Mandarin and casual gambling. He shouts numbers into his phone. Declares, *I'm rubbing the Fortune God's leg!* Misses his luck by one digit. Where there is nothing there is everything. White ointment draws greasy circles on calves.

Must be healthy. Didn't flinch.

Incredible, how a day can suddenly turn overcast and violent, as if the heavens had collapsed. Torrents of rain smash streets, threads of lightning split sky. Luminous wisps. A gigantic flash, arcing bolts leap and vanish. Relentless rain. A resounding crash.

A sunbeam on grass, a mynah bird holds wings
extended, as if in mid-flight, frozen aground.

Middle of the night. Stop sleep. When I was young, my father asked me why I was scared of ghosts, to which none of my answers satisfied. Now, as I rest, the spirit nudges my arm. *S'pore land is scarce, but they should know better than to build on hallowed ground.* I nod. The city is quiet. I want to remain in this half world, chant your name to beckon you here. Delusions, I want to trust. Enter that space where the feeling of love over-comes the love of feeling. On the fringe, I rest on my stomach, arms underneath—face in the pillow. Inhale moist cotton comfort. Don't sleep, don't wake—fear of not dreaming of you again.

Going with love is too big a burden to wear.
Man's T-shirt, Eu Tong Sen Street

Maybe I read it wrong.

In People's Park Complex, I hear the 1971 duet by Montreal band The Bells. *With all this love I have to give you, I guess I'm gonna stay with you awhile...*

It's been a long time.

My gut has a strange sensation of emptiness, despite the seafood grease feast I ate at the Plaza. Did I eat too much, or not enough?

The ghost is a *she*. She tells me that outside a temple in Tanjong Pagar there is a Chinese man dressed in black. *Go see him.*

Because fortunetellers like to wear black, lah. Even in this heat. Glad you came. Don't temple look odd between skyscrapers? Look at that incense smolder. Breathe it in. This god protect S'pore from evil. Very necessary. He guide souls to underworld, but, as you know, not all are ready to make it back. They hang on. But let's talk about you. Let me see your hands. Relax, relax. Ah, you're sensitive. Smart. Love lime-light but have hard time when public criticize you. You suffer existential sadness, drawn to occult. Must be one-of-a-kind. Under this finger you have a star—see it? Means you expressive. Career must be led by your heart. Money not important, you get what you need. The more luck you have, the more melancholic you are. Not good, not bad. Just. You know this but need another to remind you. Aiya, my hands are shaking now. I need a smoke. Don't worry. This time will be prosperous for you. You'll get there. It just takes time. Say hi to her for me.

Thieves Market, Sungei Road. I look to the elementary-colored flats at Rochor Centre, then beyond the wire fence: *State Land/No Dumping.*

Tables present jade, quartz, ammonites, petrified wood. Timepieces beam in the sun.
Arranged piles: cameras, Discmans, phones, calculators. Rusty wrenches worth saving and selling. Cotton collections, shoes, rice cookers. Vinyl handbags and pop yeh-yeh.

Trays of amulets. Plah keang—sliver of Buddha, incense ash, clay. Size like a fingernail. Malay palms place it in mine. His lips breathe *protector.* I flip aubergine bills from my back pocket. Above the canopy of trees, orange and white HDB blocks peer below encroaching dark clouds. The sun on the Rochor rainbow locates me.

Storm cracks. Tarps whip, umbrellas snap. There's nowhere to go.

Does anyone else wonder what happens to an eleven that loses a one? Is it still eleven?

What Mishima wanted: to revive the samurai spirit, to inspire and stimulate youth with a sense of order. Death in order. He didn't like that Japan's brutal side was reduced to peace and ikebana after WWII. He saw harakiri as positive, proud, opposite to the Western view of suicide, which was—in his opinion—defeat itself.

His opinion: *Harakiri makes you win.*

A farmer, face weathered from sun, hands large
with deep lines in palms. He tills earth, floods
paddies. Shoots of rice emerge. Close-up: afternoon
sun spills onto soil. Vibrations of eyeless creatures.
Contamination. Nutrients deplete. Land, a place
for corpses and ash. For mines. Mistakes. For fossils.
Secrets. Earthworms no longer plump. Soil crumbles,
lacks ingredients to hold a hill. Mud slides. Cliffs run
into rivers and that's just the start. These are just
small interruptions.

In Tofino, BC, a ghost forest. Skeletons, cedars stand in a tidal marsh. Three hundred years before, roots inundated by brackish waters. Sediments underlie. First Nations whisper a tale of devastation on a cold winter night. Cascadia undersea. Land slides. Pachena Bay, no survivors.

Below the marsh, dig. A layer of tsunami sand.

The number eleven is truly cursed. 9/11 was Chile 1973 before it was NYC. And earlier this year: March 11, 2011. Certainly, you must have felt it where you are. All those souls. Will Japan ever recover from the curse of eleven? Will we? Is it the ill-omened combination of eleven and Japan?

1 a m PST, a text from a friend: *Massive earthquake in Japan! Move to higher ground—tsunami coming!* On the TV, no tsunami warning for Vancouver, bare mention of an earthquake. Back to bed.

9 a m PST, March 11th. Horror coupled with sadness. Japan thrown a new trajectory, painful and unwanted.

My immediate reaction: fly to Japan.

Shot of shoreline. Rise and fall of ocean waves. Play
with scale. Water laps heels of running feet.

I'm sorry, I wanted to say. But to whom? And for what?

Fukushima Daiichi. Steaming mountains, wounded and wounding. Radioactive mist. A nuclear exhalation. Masao Yoshida disobeys orders, cools reactors with seawater, prevents a greater disaster, saves lives. Later given a verbal reprimand for ignoring headquarters' directives.

Waves. Seismic. Oceanic. Sonic. Nuclear. Undulating. Crippling.

The Fukushima Fifty, mostly men later in years, unlikely to bear children, stabilizers of nuclear reactors. Prepared for death, they spared younger men from the consequences of serious contamination. They embraced Bushido. Sacrifice, loyalty, honor—the warrior's way. Mishima would've admired their determination. Public paralleled them to the wandering samurai, the Forty-Seven Ronin. Ronin—*wave man.*

I shove my toe into a depression in the grass. The fresh, wet earth falls away. I kneel, press fingertips to the moist dirt. I use a rock, then my fingers, to excavate. *Possibilities*—what lies within. I burrow for faults laid in soil. With the mined earth, I sculpt a small mound.

I'm sorry that I suffer the loss of one when, at every moment, a breath is another's last. Memory is the only relationship we can have with the dead. *I'm sorry.*

There are eccentrics who foretell disasters. Their faces surface TVs and papers. When their predictions don't happen they disperse to obscurity, perhaps to reemerge later with a new premonition.

When my mind empties, it turns to you. My ethereal roommate tells me that she too longs for loved ones. She knows how I feel. I'm no longer bothered by her company. We know each other now. She cries softly, tells me that the Japanese murdered her father during the war. Even she doesn't know where they left his body. I tell her she can hold my hand but I no longer feel her presence.

Pinkie probes, unable to remove further wax. There is a blockage. I cannot alleviate the itch, even as I curette with the bamboo ear pick I bought in Chinatown. Mao tilts his head as I scour the opening of my ear with a wet facecloth.

The venue is painfully air-conditioned. Between features, writers pile napkins with complimentary curry puffs. Pastry flakes adhere to lips. They fill festival bags with free bottles of water. Compensation for enduring.

Overheard: *That author's girlfriend is a nymphomaniac.*

I look for the girlfriend.

I cast my palms on top of Mao. Wriggles tickle beneath. I want to get close, narrow my grasp until I can scoop his malleable body within my hands. I carefully slip him under an upturned glass, leave the bathroom to search for an appropriate dwelling. When I return, the glass remains inverted. Mao is nowhere to be seen.

The bathroom door is open. Mao could be any-where in the apartment. I check the inside of my shoes, under the bed, the dresser, the side table. How did he escape, and without knocking over the glass? Absorbed by the humidity? Did I actually capture him?

I need to sleep. My presentation is tomorrow, and tomorrow, reality will become a spectacle. It will be its own kind of kamikaze. All I want to talk about is the Asian predisposition to superstitions. The audience will understand. Fate, curses, numbers, death, ghosts—this is what it means to be Asian. Honor, sacrifice, revenge, filial piety.

Levi-Strauss: *Every custom or belief, however irrational, is a part of a system whose internal balance has been established over the course of centuries... teaches us one can't eliminate an element from the whole without risking destruction of the rest.*

Post-presentation, Raffles Avenue. Another star-less night. How will I navigate home without them? Instead, monster durians glitter. In view: the helix-shaped pedestrian bridge, the giant lotus, the trio of towers presenting a from-the-future canoe with the occasional burst of lasers. Encroaching drone. A herd of Lamborghinis flash a nighttime rainbow—orange, black, lime, red. A gust of exhaust. At the base of the twin-kling sky-scraped hub, below a colonial smudge, along the water's edge, the statue of the Merlion purges into the bay.

I tell them I want more than manicured: history, stories, grit. They say:

It's far.

No one goes there.

I think it's haunted.

Ah, you want to see the Ten Courts of Hell.

It closed down years ago.

Oh no, I heard they restored it.

Restored, then closed down, lah.

Why go?

Instead of determining my next project, I listen to music, eat, sleep—awaiting the muse, her inspiration. I think it's too hot for her here. I've taken to reading horoscopes for guidance. Sagittarius is suggested to 'let go.' I bet they say that to all the signs.

Maybe we should do what we're told.

Singapore, your Chinese zodiac is the snake. Snakes say little, but are wise. They're financially prosperous, but can be vain, selfish, and cheap. Although they appear to be calm, they're strong, passionate and hate to fail (so kiasu!). While Westerners consider the snake an underhanded animal, the Chinese cherish a paradox: The snake is aggression and destruction, also discretion, acumen, flexibility, and beauty.

And, my Merlion friend, you are a Leo.

Japan, while it's not easy to determine your zodiac, your Kenkoku Kinen no Hi anniversary was originally proclaimed as January 29, which was also the Lunar New Year, so the government moved it to February 11. Either date, you're an Aquarius.

Singapore, confused in its relative youth, senses a gap. Touchpoints are sacrificed for impending greatness. Proud of heritage, quick to lose it. Each visit, a new mall. Street-level sites are missing but I can't name them. They were never etched in my mind. Some were surrendered for the new circle line MRT that snakes underground. There are shields on the platform, most likely to prevent suicides. I take the train to Haw Par Villa.

I am alone with a thousand eerie statues and their principles. A rainbow of tales, a Confucian Chinese-folk paradise. Originally named Tiger Balm Gardens, the moral-fantasyland was built in 1937 by two brothers with riches earned from their popular camphor ointment. Free entry. A small treed hill. Life-sized figurines. A battle between fish-people. A snail-girl stuck in the dry earth. Armed monkeys. A colossal crab with the face of a man. A young woman breast-feeding her father-in-law.

A blanket of heat suppresses my ability to breathe. There is a Japanese word for this weather: mushiatsui.

The theme park is deserted. Is this symbolic?

I cautiously enter the dark cave that holds the gruesome Ten Courts of Hell. Lit from below, grisly scenes of souls boiled, pounded, chopped. After life. Each court, a different punishment. To misuse books results in one's body being sawn in two.

Sinners tied to posts, hearts and intestines yanked, tongues cut. Hills and trees, made of knives. In the final court, the Wheel of Reincarnation and the Wheel of Forgetfulness.